ALL THE DAYLIGHT HOURS

POEMS

AMANDA JERNIGAN
ALL THE DAYLIGHT HOURS

POEMS

Copyright © 2013 Amanda Jernigan
This edition copyright © 2013 Cormorant Books Inc.
Second Printing 2014.

No part of this publication may be reproduced, stored in a retrieval system or transmitted, in any form or by any means, without the prior written consent of the publisher or a licence from The Canadian Copyright Licensing Agency (Access Copyright). For an Access Copyright licence, visit http://www.accesscopyright.ca or call toll free 1.800.893.5777.

The publisher gratefully acknowledges the support of the Canada Council for the Arts and the Ontario Arts Council for its publishing program. We acknowledge the financial support of the Government of Canada through the Canada Book Fund (CBF) for our publishing activities, and the Government of Ontario through the Ontario Media Development Corporation, an agency of the Ontario Ministry of Culture, and the Ontario Book Publishing Tax Credit Program.

LIBRARY AND ARCHIVES CANADA CATALOGUING IN PUBLICATION

Jernigan, Amanda, 1978–
All the daylight hours / Amanda Jernigan.

Poems.
ISBN 978-1-77086-261-6

1. Title.

PS8619.E75A64 2013   C811'.6   C2013-900486-6

Excerpt from "The Pardon" from *Collected Poems 1943–2004* by Richard Wilbur. Copyright © 2004 by Richard Wilbur. Reprinted by permission of Houghton Mifflin Harcourt Publishing Company. All rights reserved.
Excerpt from *The Horse's Mouth* by Joyce Cary. First published in Great Britain by Michael Joseph Ltd in 1944. Reprinted by permission of the Andrew Lownie Agency, for the Estate of Joyce Cary.
Excerpt from "The Trees" from *The Complete Poems of Philip Larkin* by Philip Larkin, edited by Archie Burnett. Copyright © 2012 by The Estate of Philip Larkin. Reprinted by permission of Faber and Faber Ltd and Farrar, Straus and Giroux, LLC.

Cover art and design: Angel Guerra/Archetype
Wood engravings © John Haney
Cover image: Pierre Coupey, *Notations 28*, 2002 (detail). Oil on canvas over panel.
70 x 45 in. / 177.8 x 114.3 cm. Corporate collection, Vancouver. http://www.coupey.ca/
Interior text design: Tannice Goddard, Soul Oasis Networking
Printer: Sunville Printco

Printed and bound in Canada.

CORMORANT BOOKS INC.
390 Steelcase Road East, Markham, Ontario, L3R 1G2
www.cormorantbooks.com

for John and Anson

Contents

1 A Natural Day

The Bather *5*
After "Inversnaid" *6*
Lullaby *7*
The Hyll *8*
A Natural Day *9*
Dos-à-dos *10*
Death and Taxes *11*
Counting Rhyme *12*
Rushlight *13*
Shelter *14*
Holy *15*
Telemachy *16*
Elegy at Jolicure *18*
Impasse *19*
Memoir *20*

2 Through the Pass

The Watch of the Third King *25*
Milan *27*
The Marble King of Athens, Greece *28*
Beasts *30*
Horse and Train *31*
Bats *32*
Favourite *33*
The Sword of Damocles *34*

Tricks Bid and Made in No Trump   35
Reflection   36
Aperture   37
Writ   38
Advice   39
Ply   41

3 Along the Fence-line

When the Weather Comes
(Poems for St John's, Newfoundland)
  i Arrival   47
  ii The Ice   48
  iii Anglican Cemetery   49
  iv Summer Solstice   50
  v Georgestown Bakery   51
  vi December   52

Desire Lines
(Poems for Terra Nova National Park)
  i Exclosure   53
  ii Boardwalk   54
  iii Prescribed Burn   56
  iv Park Harbour   57
  v Bear   58

Cynosure   59
Impresario   60
Hello Wounded Soldiers   62
Clearcut   63
Arbor Vitae   64
The Bookworm Riddle   65
Daubers   66
On Modern Verse   67
Routine   68
Octavo   69
Love Letter   70
Cleaning Out the Barn   71

4 The Slippery Air

    Speak   *77*
    Spring   *78*
    May 31st   *79*
    Blackout   *80*
    Static Prelude   *81*
    Poem with the Gift of a Timepiece   *82*
    Grandfather Clock   *83*
    Nursery Rhyme   *84*
    Marrying Days   *85*
    Rings   *86*
    Epithalamium   *87*
    Encounter   *88*
    Scale   *89*
    Love Poem   *90*
    What Is, Goes   *91*

    Notes   *93*

    List of Wood Engravings   *95*

    Acknowledgements   *97*

    About the Author   *99*

I

A Natural Day

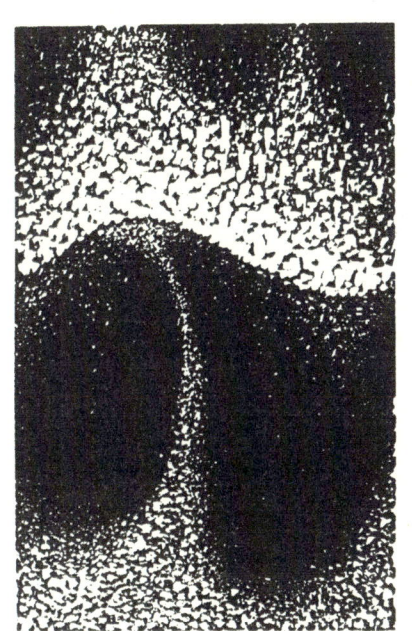

The Bather

The lake (*Wishing ever to sunder
Things and things' selves* ...) took down
the trees in all their detail, held up
the light in its descent; it broke
the bather at the water line.
As long as she could hold her breath
she watched through leaded glass: the sun,
rose to the water's window, rose.

After "Inversnaid"

Ash in dark water becomes a bright net.
What is it catching? Wildness and wet.
Where would we be without wildness and wet?
What will the world be, once bereft?

Lullaby

My little lack-of-light, my swaddled soul,
December baby. Hush, for it is dark,
and will grow darker still. We must embark
directly. Bring an orange as the toll
for Charon: he will be our gondolier.
Upon the shore, the season pans for light,
and solstice fish, their eyes gone milky white,
come bearing riches for the dying year:
solstitial kingdom. It is yours, the mime
of branches and the drift of snow. With shaking
hands, Persephone, the winter's wife,
will tender you a gift. Born in a time
of darkness, you will learn the trick of making.
You shall make your consolation all your life.

The Hyll

It is an old door banging in this April wind:
an apple turns to earth; a wave takes flight;
the fir trees stop their sighs to listen.
All the songs of Orpheus say one of these two things:
either, life is the end of death or, death is the end of life.

Some say, on her return from Hades, Orpheus broke
her harp for splits, and gave up song for medicine;
others, once she'd seen the Styx,
the boatman's ferry creaking with its legions of incurables,
she traded in her stethoscope for a lyre. Both are true.

There was a hyll, and on the hyll a verie levell
plot, fayre greene with grass. There I awoke,
and struggled to put language to
the empty place in memory *that silts with words / of closure,*
looking for words that might yet keep it open.

A Natural Day

The day after your father's wake
I walk a circle around the field
where last week you and I made love,
wading in through goldenrod
and Joe-pye weed and Queen Anne's lace
and brome until we found ourselves concealed.
Since then, the weeds have all leapt up:
*Ile leape up to my God: who pulles
me doune* — I consider breasting them,
but I know the spot is overgrown.
It's foolishness to think that I,
even if space could stand for time,
even if you were with me, love,
could find it.

Dos-à-dos

We settle down to sleep at night,
affectionate, facing one another,

or torso fast to torso pressed
as if our hearts could speak together.

Mornings, we wake back to back.

However much we love, there's something
in us always turns away.

Let us forgive this in each other.
We can make it up by day.

Death and Taxes

Here together we are wholly
love's, and I forget that *"Noli
me tangere,"* Wyatt's fable
insisting we are all on loan —

Caesar's warning not reserved for courtly
lovers: we are wild, as we are mortal.

If love's currency's debased
by death's impression on the face,
while there's breath in us we're able
to render unto each its own.

Counting Rhyme
    after Catullus

    Come live with me and be my love,
    and let's not give the time of day
    to those who say we're mad. The sun,
    once set, can rise and cheat the grave:
    you and I, once dead, are done.
    Nox est perpetua …, as they say.
    Kiss me a thousand times, a hundred,
    then another thousand, then
    another hundred, thousand, hundred —
    with so many kisses we'll lose track,
    so no one, counting them, can take them back.

Rushlight
We two alone will sing like birds i' th' cage ...

It is not easy, however half
in love we are with easeful death,
to sing by rushlight in a cage
of rushes that diminishes
with every breath; nor yet to leave

off singing — taking for a stage
direction the prompter's whispered *Love,
and be silent*, to swallow Cordelia's
line and exit — however half
in love we are with fretful life.

Shelter

Out in the fields Lear rages, stamping out
the frozen clods, matching the elements bellow
for blow, until he scarcely knows himself
from Old Man Winter. He reaches up then brings
his fists down pounding on his chest as if he means
to dash the light from the very stars.

Inside the barn, the myth, unswaddled, proves
a bare fork'd thing. Yet we will keep
with this philosopher, who stands in his skivvies like the bold
new year, eulogizing winter in a voice that cracks:
"the oldest hath borne most, we that are young
shall never see so much nor live so long."

Death by death, the play sharpens down towards winter.
This last speech, and then, for all Kent says
"Break heart, I prithee, break," the lights come up.
Applauding, we hold hovels in our hands, and the year
sharpens down towards winter. Heart breaks not.
Between our births and deaths we but continue

to invent. Inside the barn, we hear the clapping
of unfastened board. The light comes up, and briefly
this bare room out-shelters stable, and the wind
out-hallelujahs angelsong; and even that
bright annual, that star that bloomed on Christmas Eve,
may be outshone by our perennial sun.

Holy

The words the weight of a stylus only,
travelling the surface slip
of clay, make slight impressions when
you hear them first. Repeated, they
cleave to the groove. This is the source
of faith; the words ring true. When Hamlet
walks on stage, act three, scene one,
the audience inhales en masse
and mouths, "To be, or not to be …."
Thus, even unbelieving, I
recite in earnest, "And it came to pass
in those days that there went out a decree
from Caesar Augustus." Travelling home,
we likewise cleave to roads we know,
and in our minds the tracks are laid
for these small houses letting go
of smoke, these rivers clenched
in ice, these pockmarked signs,
and whether there's a child or not,
the roads run thick with traffic, lines
of people going to be counted.

Telemachy

> *The child is father of the man;*
> *And I could wish my days to be*
> *Bound each to each by natural piety.*

Sound of the foghorn, off. The scene, a rocky coast.
The fog is in so low it seems the tuckamore
have taken root in it, finding better purchase there
than in the peat and sandstone underneath.
Through this inverted forest we tramp like gods, our boots
displacing crackerberry constellations, sending
spiders shuttling at their astrolabical webs.
Perhaps it is the topsy-turviness of things
that has me recollecting Wordsworth's line "The child
is father of the man"; this, and the fact I'm hiking
with my brother, astonished at the thoughtful man
the thoughtful ten-year-old I used to know has reared.

Sound of the foghorn, off. I try to count the blasts —
a vessel underway sounds one prolonged blast
every two minutes, a vessel underway but stopped
sounds two, and so forth — but I lose track, and find myself
instead arranging in the intervals long, paratactic
sentences from Lattimore's translation of *The Odyssey:*
and the men quickly went aboard and sat to the oarlocks
and sitting well in order dashed their oars in the grey sea ....
The child is father of the man. The story of Odysseus
begins with Telemachos. For the one to have his homecoming,
the other must go to sea: *into Sparta and to sandy Pylos*
to ask after his dear father's homecoming, if he can hear something ....

Sound of the foghorn, off. A vessel towing, a cableship
at work, a fishing vessel engaged in fishing, a vessel
commandless, all of these would issue one prolonged
and two short blasts. Perhaps it is the signal

at the lighthouse, then. Built in nineteen fifty-one,
that pyramidal wooden tower, painted red
and white, stands at the entrance to the narrows. Which is also
the exit, of course. The path drops sharply ahead of me.
My brother turns to wait. Here in the shelter of the trees
it's calm, but we can hear the wind encountering the cliff-face
to our right and, below, *the wash of the breakers,* wave on wave
bound each to each, in what I suppose is natural piety.

Sound of the foghorn, off, the lighthouse: calling the one man
home to port, calling the other out to sea.

Elegy at Jolicure

The wind rolls itself out, and weather comes
like the expected emperor. Only the scattered house maintains
it isn't ocean here.

The leaves of the chestnut tree are down; you will not
rake them up. Until you couldn't, you maintained
your house against this gravity.

We wake, we start the coffee pot, we dress
ourselves in motley. Only our elegies maintain
it isn't ocean here.

Impasse

Sei allem Abschied voran: half

a line from Rilke's *Die Sonette*
an Orpheus as my motto,

I rehearsed my elegiac art
("be in advance of all parting")

and won, I thought, with each song deeper,
until I stood before the keeper

in whom I've come to recognize myself.

Memoir

I thought about a narrow road.
At length, it stretched before me.
I travelled it, unravelled it:
it seemed to ravel from me.

At first it was a simple line
and then it was a circuit
and then it seemed to spiral inwards —
farther still I took it.

It seemed to lengthen under me.
It offered no encounter.
Diminishing circumferences
contracted to a centre.

I found a mighty crossroads there,
twelve byways intersecting.
I set up as a customs guard,
a heavy toll collecting.

Now days and nights I've bided here,
and sometimes I imagine
I'm coextensive with the web,
so close its oscillation.

Myself become circumference,
attending radii
within, and at my centre something
tugging like a fly.

2

Through the Pass

The Watch of the Third King

These slow nights in the desert I can almost hear
the rough beast moving its thighs. My brothers
lie asleep. Before their lips I hold the glass
of heaven. Stars prick my eyes. Our animals chaw
and huff and shift position. I listen to the whistle
of the architect of dunes: far off across the sands,
he's rearranging. I make of my hands an hourglass
and night flows uninterrupted into day.

This cockatoo remembers: my own kingdom.
The sun was like the bells on the morning's wrists.
In the garden, I would greet the hubble-bubblers
and the takers of the air. A tethered camel
turned a wheel to draw the water. She paused, once,
in her round, to turn her besotted face on me.
Such moments are child enough. What can I bear them?

My brothers, I love your opalescent blisters.
I love the sweet bald pates beneath your crowns.
Let me unroll for you this dusty carpet.
Let me relieve you of your frankincense and gold.
This Matthew says that being warned of God
in a dream that we should not return to Herod
we departed to our own country another way.
He does not mention that one of us was driven
to distraction, and wandered off across the dunes,
and wept before the children of the nomads.

He says we seek a child, upon whose shoulders,
scarcely broader than his head, we'll lay the burden
of our worship. I'll tell the truth to this green bird:
it matters less and less to me if we reach

the stable. Enough, for me, the creatures' breath,
the dust that clots our palms until we cannot
tell the love-line from the life-line. A bright star
took a liking to us outside of Borj el-Khadra.
Sometimes, like a yellow dog, it follows us,
and sometimes, like a yellow dog, it leads us on.

Milan

Out of air, out of thin air,
without a rack to conjure with: "The cloud-
capped towers, the gorgeous palaces, the solemn
temples …" he tries, but none appear.

"Be cheerful," says his dresser, Cal: "Our ends
are now unravelled. These our spirits, as I
foretold you, were all actors and are melted — I mean,
are flown, off to the bar. Lift up thy

feet." *So dusty men will sweep the floor
of even the great globe itself: we are
such stuff* …, thinks Prospero. "Okay —" says Cal.

But Prospero is balanced, still, on the island
of his vanity. "Tempest," he whispers
to himself, and lo, a breath of air.

The Marble King of Athens, Greece

Mibless, he borrowed his first shooter —
from the son of an air-force man, who loaned
it grudgingly and lived to rue it —
then captured every marble he would own.
The local urchins, army brats,
suspendered sons of diplomats,
in the Attic sun they knuckled down
and played for keeps.

Knock a marble from the ring,
keep the marble, shoot again.
Hit your partner's taw instead,
and take his mibs for he is dead.

He tallied up his victories:
the swirls and aggots, steelies, all
those cat's-eyes, crystals, potteries,
those corns and big dough-rollers,
an embarrassment of riches. Now
he spills them out to see them, how
each one contains in its keel
a scrap of light.

Now he consigns them to their sack.
He trusts them to a steamer chest
of linens which, by luggage rack
of army jeep, is taken to the *USS*
America. The crossing takes
a week. Back home, when he unpacks
the chest, he rifles through the sheets
and finds them gone.

Were they stolen by a docker?
Or taken as a tar's reward
and anted up in steerage poker?
Or by a guileful cabin steward
as ransom for this voyage to his son?
Perhaps just lost. Well, he won
them once and he can win them over
again, he thinks. In dreams, however,

he sees the satchel, sinking, helped
undone by currents, sow its prize
in coral reefs and groves of kelp
till those that were his pearls are eyes.

Beasts
> *In my kind world the dead were out of range*
> *And I could not forgive the sad or strange*
> *In beast or man....*
>   — Richard Wilbur, "The Pardon"

He told me of the Cape-Town walkup where
he lived till he was eight; the years spent there,
he claims, his best,

although he'd range his wooden beasts, some nights,
along the windowsill to watch the fights
outside. At last,

presumably, his folks were reconciled
to moving — this no place to raise a child —
and made to flee.

The family came to Canada, where not
much happens for a lion or an ocelot
or boy to see —

where I grew up, and entertained myself
with fairy tales from which I'd struck the wolf,
though now, I've found,

I summon wolf and lion, woman, Lord
knows what, and bid that wooden horde
to laager round.

Horse and Train
for Mogul, recollected

I would not go with lumber, nor with flats of rutabagas, nor
   with nickel from the States,
but with these creatures, compound of the shrubbery of Africa,
   I'd travel.

That chimps might strut and fret before the people of Vancouver,
they would take the circus through the pass, the *Herald* said.

Each boxcar bore a painting of a trotting horse, in varied pose,
all gussied for the ring. I'd sussed them out. The train left early.

At five, I jigged a lock and let me in. I thought my boxcar-mate
   a horse.
Was only when the rattleslats let through first light I saw his
   convict garb

and knew him zebra. I lay me back on hay and dung, and woke
   past dawn,
ears popping. The alpine light stabbed in between the boards,

made glint the gunky eyes of beast and man,
and glaciers were unsettled by the gibes of gibbons.

When I pressed my face against the slats, the fissures gave
   on facing peaks,
on dizzy cliffs, on drop-offs that would cow a petrel.

The trumpet of an elephant made shiver the mountain's flank.
I saw, zootropic, as we took a hairpin turn and doubled back,
   the tailing train.

The boxcar horse had found his legs and made to gallop.

Bats

They billow from a hillside in Cha-am.
Together, they are more than plural:
the planet's darkest song, a tongue,
a serpent muscling air apart,
a dire banner come unfurled,
a river flowing wholly from
the old, mute mountain's desperate heart,
the last confession of the world.
Conceive of each one singly, if you can.

Favourite

He gave his youngest concubine, to keep,
a golden falcon captured in mid-dive,
its diamond-crusted talons poised to rake
the hide of cringing hind, or any creature,
its rubied craw emitting silent shriek:
enough to wake the dead, if not to wake
the king — the king is taken out of nature.

But that was long ago and one must make
one's peace. She keeps the statue under lock
and key, of course: it's only prudent. Guest
to her modest, second-storey flat, you'll look
in vain for hood or glove that might bespeak
the present of her concubinal past,
the eyas stooping on her mind in sleep.

The Sword of Damocles
Fortunatus sibi Damocles videbatur.

Indeed it was a rare device:
the king's august assembly sees
before them hapless Damocles
finger the grapes like loaded dice;

above, attendant on a trice
and poised to smash his plate and pate
there hangs, incorporated fate,
the sword of Dionysius.

They howled to see me gotten good.
But now it's late. The crowd has gone.
The servingmen have all withdrawn,
taking the plates of untouched food.

I'm left conversing with the blade:
I burden it with my confession,
made a tyrant's object lesson.
I nod off in its meagre shade.

But Dionysius should know
the greater trick were to persuade
one's subject that his foe's the blade,
lest he should think to steal the show.

If not for fear I'd spring the trap
I might, in fact, be moved to laugh,
composing here my epitaph,
Damocles thought himself very happy.

Tricks Bid and Made in No Trump

i   I broke the news: a total rout.
     Her Majesty was quite put out
     and went straight off to reprimand
     the king, left me to play her hand.

ii   Deal out the cards. I cannot force
     your hand, but I can play. Of course,
     you made my way where e'er I went,
     O handsomest impediment.

iii   How can you ask I take the verdict
     silently? Your double aspect
     signals what the cards erased.
     A story is but fate outfaced.

iv   The wind is riffling the shingles
     overhead. We play the angles,
     build a house of cards instead.
     Take up the harp. The king is dead.

v   The dealer, keen to raise the stakes,
     has cut the deck to twenty-six.
     I seize the alphabetic grace
     and cut my losses, play the ace.

Reflection

The swan slipped under the bridge — a palmed card,
a dropped coin, a swaddled child, delivered
or abandoned — a surreptitious movement,
but scandalously bright, and we could hardly
feign not having seen it. I thought about
Macpherson's swan, white habited; and Baudelaire's,
an exile from its *lac natal;* the snow-
white somnatational swans of Outram's
"Ms Cassie by Tarnished Water": dying
swans sing sweetest, Brecht maintained. But Brewer
tells us swans aren't known to sing. The sirens,
too, were silent, according to Kafka. Truer
words were never spoken, never taken
back. In your negative the swan is black.

Aperture

The pond's perfected surface begged us,
"Let me lie or leave your mark
on me." At first we left in silence.
We then returned and lobbed the stone
that made the aperture in ice
in which are sourced those synapsed fractures.
We then returned and said, "It is
a wheel within a wheel. It is
an eye in winter. It is the hole
in the heart stopped up by the perfect image."
For we by vision are struck dumb.
And we are struck articulate.

Writ

I've struggled to pronounce as if my own
those twenty syllables, your thrush's charm:
*O fret not after knowledge — I have none,
and yet my song comes native with the warmth.*
Perrault recounts the story of a woman
who spoke in flowers, envy of the kings,
her gift a version of the poet's dream,
to utter no ideas but in things —
and yet this is a kind of death in life.
As no one knew so well as you, perhaps,
who struggled to pronounce as if your own
the spring, till roses tumbled from your lips
(O fret not after beauty — I have none)
so actual they stained your handkerchief.

Advice

i   Discretion must be exercised
in the use of Charts.
They must not be regarded
as *infallible*, as we have shown.
I have on good authority
from old salts down in Hearts
Content these soundings:
but the lines are far
apart from one another and
admit the possibility
of the existence of unknown
isolated dangers.

ii   Again, a Chart
or Logbook may
be accurate
when printed,
but wind

       up unreliable due
to changes in shoals
and buoys and lights —
to say nothing of wind

       and the author's emendations.

iii   Words may get adrift.
Like other exposed seamarks they
are liable to injury,

                                   [...]

destruction by sea or tempest as,

Four fathom five thy father lies ...

Your full reliance must not be placed

upon them.

iv   Go down you blood red roses, go down.
Oh, you pinks and posies —
Go down you blood red roses, go down.

Ply

On deck the tars had leave to talk
so long as they were spinning. Tale
and twine were thus entangled: language
tends to twinning. So tutored
by his fingers, the yarning sailor knew
how words, like wool, must be perplexed
if they're to clothe a truth. At times
he'd see a skein of seabirds streaming
towards the spindle, or feel the sea
itself perplexed as the vessel turned
to ply, or hear the steersman's wheel
and know, for all its to's and fro's
it spoke, in turn, of revolution —
then would the deck beneath his feet
seem treadle to the great wheel of the sun.

3

Along the Fence-line

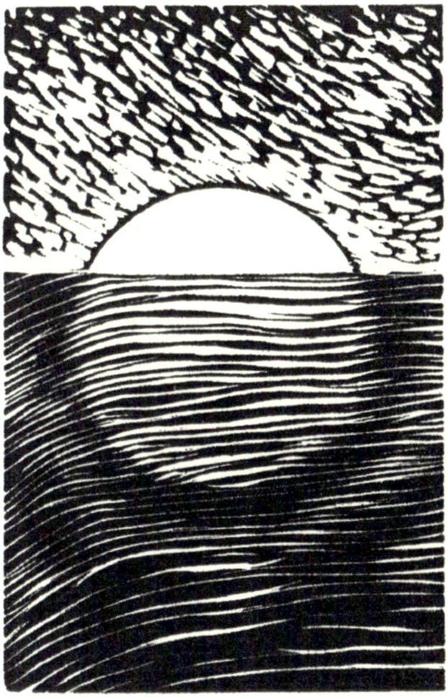

When the Weather Comes
(Poems for St. John's, Newfoundland)

i Arrival

>We arrive abruptly. The highway coughs us up
>in bog, among the flat black pools that brood in peat, the tracks
>of moose, mosquitoes, boulders scattered like a fist of jacks,
>
>and spits us into the face of a ship in dry dock — down
>to the city. Along the precipitous streets are stacked,
>like cracker boxes, clapboard houses — up, now,
>
>provision your soul. We see the tower tossing
>several hills away, a matchbox ship,
>and all around the city heaves, unfathomed.

ii The Ice

>Overnight the ice ships out:
>by daylight it's a rime
>on the horizon; time
>was, you'd go to sleep,
>ships berthed six-deep
>in the harbour, convoyed,
>wake to find them gone —
>each the other's image, yet
>the tidy metaphor
>obscures some third
>thing, thought or feeling moored
>at poem's beginning, massing
>in those opening lines, missing
>by its end.

iii Anglican Cemetery

At last the sea delivers up the sun;
the light files in among the vandalled stones and all
the angels stand up to be counted: one extends

a wounded hand; one wanders blindly; one
puts up a stump of arm to block the light; and one ascends,
its trailing fingers loosed to let us fall.

iv Summer Solstice

The juggler has been practising:
he keeps that goldenmost ball, some days,
so long in the sky we fool ourselves
into thinking it won't ever come down.

Thick haze above the harbour now:
for June is mostly smoke and mirrors,
fog above a steely sea.
"The sun's up there somewhere," we say.

Some evenings when we've come to least
expect it we have seen it land,
unlooked-for, where he said it would,
in the juggler's outstretched hand.

v Georgestown Bakery

Wednesday morning, cold as a bell,
grey as a church, we take ourselves
to the Georgestown bakery; bakery smells
collide with the conventual air.

Bread-pans powdering the floor,
geraniums baking on the sill:
these things take small account of us.

Outside, the snow, half-hearted, falls.
The ovens' breath obscures the glass,
and heaped loaves comfort wooden shelves.

vi December

December sets up house again
in the old familiar quarter,
and pushes the table out from the wall
and lays in rum and porter,
and splits some kindling for the stove,
and when the weather comes,
all the daylight hours crowd
into her small rooms.

Desire Lines
(Poems for Terra Nova National Park)

i Exclosure

    Exactly that I wanted most
    to write about I would enclose,
    with chicken wire, driven post:
    knowing how words are wont to browse
    on birch and alder, apse and var,
    and so completely to revise
    one's subject (pin cherry, chuckley pear,

    in the winter of the year).

    I follow the runs of snowshoe hare
    that go along the fence-line here.
    The saplings have grown up at last:
    indeed, so thick I can't see past
    their greening ranks, and must surmise
    what I have managed to enclose,
    a paradise, or a paradise lost.

ii Boardwalk

Three-leaved false
Solomon's seal,
speckled alder,
sedge, sweet gale,
lady's slipper,
leatherleaf,
laurel, rhodora,
labrador tea,
black spruce,
sphagnum moss,
cotton grass,
corn lily,
partridgeberry,
chuckley pear,
alder, larch,
juniper,
crackerberry,
stiff club moss,
hurts, worts,
rosemary:
the words
are stubborn, brook
few rhymes;
verse will not take,
although the bog
is braided
with desire lines;

milled, however,
cut, and laid
along alliterative stringers
side by each,
the common names
may yet afford
a kind of walkway: lead
you far out over
the wetland, never
let you touch it.

iii Prescribed Burn

In flagrante delicto the fire
rejoiceth as a giant to run its course

(far off, I wrote, the kindled hills
resemble the clumps of red-stemmed moss
that we'll find growing in the burn
among the ranks of firekills
years from now, when we return)

leaping the blackline of my verse.

iv Park Harbour

> The terns fish the bay. From here
> the outlet is obscured behind
> a spit of land, and so this inlet
> seems to be their private pool,
> to centre on some point below
> the centres of the untrue loops
> they circumscribe in staggered flights
> above the heaps of knotted wrack,
> the naked rocks, the sunken pier,
> within the larger circle of
> the spruce- and balsam-wooded drums
> that form the shore, likewise untrue
> (all this will burn within the year).
> What startles me completely as
> the first felt motion of a babe
> in utero is how that bird
> can drop mid-circumscription, here
> at poem's end, and pluck a silver
> herring from the middle.

v Bear

We came around the corner just
in time to see the daylight dis-
appearing, into the ambling blackness
of the biggest bear we'd ever
seen. The light; the sandy road,
its shoulders blanketed with moss;
the alders wading hip-deep in
the ditches; and the dusty spruce,
the deckle edges of these woods:
these things and all the names for them,
the things that we compare them to,
emptied as a single stream
into the darkness of that bear
who just then turned his massive head
around, in time, to see us.

Cynosure
for Winston, a she-dog

My paunch is apposite. My tail is swag.
My pupils are a pair of brandied currants.
The lappets of my ears entice
the slob-mouthed hounds of Sackville.
I am aloof. I've bigger fish to fry.

I am the cynosure, the wolf refined.
In turning at a scent I am an eddy.
I've badgered out the deepest earths
where never tarried terrier;
gave Cerberus — all three of him — the eye.

Impresario

On his smoke-break outside STRUTS,
under the damoclean sign,
sporting his signature hood and hunch,
Paul looks as if he might await
the post, the bus, the forecast rain,
perhaps the Revelation. I can't
imagine any of these would faze him.

If a Westfalia van pulled up
discharging seven angels with
their vials and seals and plagues and trumps,
feeling it's not advisable
to billet these gentlemen at the farm,
he might direct them to the nearest
campsite, thinking, *Rockstars*.

If Wallace Stevens' glass equipage
came direct from Connecticut,
rattling on about poetry
and blackbirds for the umpteenth time,
he might remind the driver of
the upcoming deadline for Council grants
and tell him there is wireless at Ducky's.

If the last red tide swept up
from Fundy, inundating Lorne,
turning the Roadhouse to pickup sticks,
he might just snuff his cigarette
and swing a leg over his bike,
cycling leisurely back home
to check on the sod wall. Maybe.

Still nights at the farm the stars
don't land but keep on going, to their summer
feeding grounds, perhaps to morning.
Paul's out in the unmown yard
feeding the fire with old scrap wood
hauled out from the still-plumb barn
for (while Rome fiddles) burning.

Hello Wounded Soldiers

I shouldn't have been at all surprised to see you —
having soft-shoed past the duty-nurse,
a vaudeville standup, in your day-job three-piece —
fumbling through the hospital drapes. Of course.

This, after all, is the man who wrenched his stomach
(and possibly also other, unmentionable parts)
descending from the South Side Hills, last summer,
rather than scuttle a bucket of late-season hurts.

A man must look to his berries. And his friends.
Which likewise are thin on the ground, and beyond price.
Which is why, days later, hospital long behind us,
our answering machine still greets us in your voice

(the message you left while we were in Emerg,
re-saved): *Hello wounded soldiers, this is George ...*

Clearcut

It pleases us to think the sun
redeems the logging roads with cane,
with high cicadan orisons,
with fern and black-eyed Susan.

Picking our way amid the slash
we say blackberry rosaries,
we finger their knotted beadwork, one
for the bucket one for me, as in
he loves me not he loves me.

Watching where we eat our prayers,
the trees themselves might pity us.
When autumn comes they lose their leaves
by accident, deciduous.

Arbor Vitae

i   With this ring
the bark thee-weds
the heartwood
every year anew.

The birch knows
in its bones what we
perennially
discover:

the past is strong,
it lends us structure,
but life is in
the cambium, the now.

ii   Confounding the chronologist,
the maple's numeration puts
for each year a concentric cipher,
summing centuries to nought.

This seconds what the cosmos teaches:
all the great imperfect hum
of life puts up but faint resistance
in between ashes and ashes, dust and dust.

iii   The rings are fictions of the kerf,
however. We coin them where we cleave.

Midsummer, master founder, pours,
in the mould of a living beech, a living beech.

The Bookworm Riddle
after the Old English of the Exeter Book

A moth ate words. It struck me,
when I heard it, as a kind of wonder:
that a worm should swallow a poet's song
(a thief in the dark), her fixed address,
along with its bastion. Familiar bandit,
none the richer for its plunder.

Daubers

> *[He] asked me what had happened to the world which had ceased to admire such real "true" art, and allowed itself to be cheated by "daubers" who could neither draw nor glaze; who dared not attempt "finish."*
> — *Joyce Cary,* The Horse's Mouth

As a prince, once brought to bay,
will run on his sword before he's borne
in triumph off, each son that's born
runs on himself, so dies each day

as we were promised. Like a diver
taking aim at his own likeness,
so decreed his royal highness:
ye shall cast into the river.

So we take the wailing babe
and strap him to the ark of form,
leave him bobbing on the foam:
daubed with slime and pitch, but saved.

On Modern Verse

Humbly built a house of blocks,
and nothing could be neater.
He looked askance at Mumbly's mess
and called the man a cheater.

Mumbly gave the house a kick
and said the scatter's sweeter:
houses are for bourgeoisie
and so are rhyme and metre.

Humbly built the house again
and glued the blocks together,
and threw the house at Mumbly's head
to show him form is better.

Routine

"The world of publishing," you told
me on my first day on the job, "is mad.
Well — what did you expect?
There is no money in it: what we've sold
this summer wouldn't buy you lunch,
which is what editors are out to — in both senses.
Authors? Unavoidable expenses.
Printers? An eccentric bunch,
but mostly daft (myself excepted).
One more thing: the public doesn't read."

All this no doubt intended to dissuade.
Instead, intrigued (and obstinate) I stayed —
and saw, against the fickle post,
which might bring money or disaster,
there was coffee at exactly ten o'clock,
the local gossip at the dairy, toasted
sandwiches in paper bags, and last
year's bulbs reliably emerging. And though
we were behind, the press would slow
unfailingly at four, for Simba's walk.

You've been typecast (excuse the pun)
quixotically: on pressback, Zephyr
Antique laying waste forever
to shoddy bindings, box-stores, bills.
Yet I have seen this battle done
with neither swords nor slings — nor quills.

On Friday nights you swept the shopfloor clean.
Against the wrack of publishing, the sanity of routine.

Octavo

One, thrice folded, gives us eight
leaves, sixteen pages: freight
sufficient for a printer's sheet.
The sixth leaf makes the third complete;
the first is married to the last:
we read the present in the past
though, pages cut, all seems to be
related chronologically.
Have I seemed to praise, ab ovo,
in itself, this fine octavo?
Praise it as a preface, rather,
sewn and gathered to another.

Love Letter

One wants one's words to catch the light
that warms the page one's writing on.
I love you as meltwater loves
the channels into which it flows.

Must I use *one*, instead of *I*?
Perhaps tomorrow, reading this,
you'll notice how the daylight pools
in the formal hollows of those o's.

Cleaning Out the Barn
Sie liessen immer Raum.

We've swept the mouse shit from the corners,
pitched the fork with the broken tines
and stacked the wood: you could get married
or act out a nativity
in here: ... *a manger for a bed,*
because the innkeep had no room.

I don't know how to leave no room:
the unicorn may lift its head,
but god will not be courted by
an empty barn, a port in air.
Fill up the measure of your lines.
Outside the poem the child is born.

4

The Slippery Air

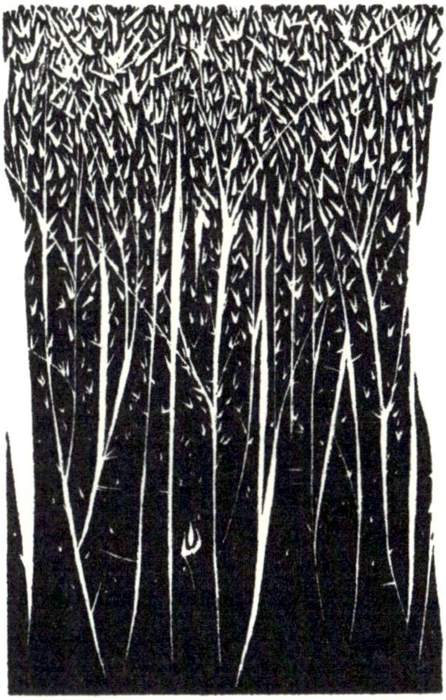

Speak

After the accident you spoke with her by phone,
but by the time you got there she had gone
into a coma: a darkened house she'd leave

by the back door. In all these years I've never
asked the question. I used to think it was,
Of what did you speak? And then I thought it was,

What did you speak. Now, it seems, the query
has resolved itself into this imperative
directed at myself, a wonderstone.

Spring

The trees are coming into leaf
Like something almost being said ...
   — Philip Larkin, "The Trees"

There's nothing "almost" about the way
   the trees are coming into leaf:
they've spoken; however, what they say
   is in a language other than
the one this poem almost speaks.

May 31st

The crabapple tree is abandoned
to bloom, the sky to blue, the barn-
boards to the weather. Try
as I might to abandon myself
to work, I hear you splitting
wood. You've lost your father.

Blackout

Wartime, the city under blackout, you had to trust
that what you'd seen by day would be enough
to help you find your way by night, dead reckoning down Water Street,
to the place where the laneway ended, the right door opened.

Exactly so I've seen you feel your way along
a line of verse, inserting *something something*
for the trochees that you knew were there, until you reached the rhyme-word
at the end. Now, of course, the city

is under blackout. What we know now of your life
is all we'll ever know: we have to trust
that it's enough to help us find our way down *something something* streets
to the place where something ends and something opens.

Static Prelude

That brief subsiding crackle
at the first touch of the needle, *tout:*
contained in it all breath, all sound divining.

Though retrospect ascribes to it
the character of song, perhaps,
it is for now itself, beyond our kenning.

The white noise of the universe,
which might go on forever, might
diminish, just in time for a beginning.

Poem with the Gift of a Timepiece

Time keeps its watch upon your pulse;
your pulse may keep a watch on time,

so let this be upon your wrist:

hold up, against its perfect rhyme
that which is slant, and off, and else.

Grandfather Clock

In childhood I was lulled to sleep
by your untitled numbers: clock,
given that all we do is lose
time — the decades stream from us
like water (as my father says)
off ducks' backs — it is marvellous
that we've designed, in tick and talk,
these mechanisms that can keep it.

Nursery Rhyme

Isla lies at last asleep.
Yellow ducks are on her cap.
Ducks, for all their jollity,
do not exist for Isla yet.

Light and dark are mysteries,
let alone her hands and feet.
One and two, awake asleep.
We, and the world, and ducks, can wait.

Marrying Days

These, my friends, are marrying days.
One afternoon last summer I saw
my childhood orchard fortress made
a wedding bower, and my erstwhile
ally of those boy-girl wars go bearing
the white standard, happily, to hold
a parley with the gentleman opposed.

Two other friends, in March, took hands
and swore, in the parlance of our times,
to live together, after Customs
and Immigration's ordinance,
in the holy estate of modern love,
and in so doing named each other
person and person, if not man and wife.

Now you. I wonder: what words
will you choose to be the footmen
of your vows, of all words? In what costume
will you wed? What dignitaries will preside
at this your co-ordainment? To whom
shall I address this poem? To whom
it may concern: that is, to you.

May you be, not of one mind, but mindful
of each other; not of one flesh, but, fleshly,
may you delight in one another.
May you be, not of one heart, but heartily
in love for all your days; and may
we count among your blessings ever
this your love not born but made.

Rings

The ring, a metal token
whose geometry contrives
to recollect our loves to us
thereby conjoining lives:

tall order for a figure
whose simplicity belies
time's will to ring the changes
on the strongest "thou-and-I."

The metaphor can bear it.
Consider: when it dives,
a right whale fashions rings enough
to marry sea and sky.

Epithalamium

Ovid, who sang of the beautiful changes,
changed a desert to a grove
with the lovely Latin names
of maple, myrtle, linden, fir.
Sparrows stopped their songs to hear;
stags stood rooted to the ground;
even the poets forgot to prey
on one another at the sound,
and formed a breathless circle there.
I should invoke his name today,
to help me fill the slippery air
with verses worthy of your love.
It would be useless. Where we are
the words themselves fall silent, gather round.

Encounter

A friend, seeing his babe in ultrasound,
imagined it an astronaut, *behind*
glass dome reflections, lost in space ...,
and so I had that image close to mind
when the technician finally tipped her screen
to me, revealing — not an astronaut, but Earth,
so "small, light blue, so touchingly alone."
Thus Leonov. It was a commonplace,
back then, that once we had the earth in sight,
the isolation of the planet "known,"
we would clean up our act, would mend our ways —
a kind of cosmic recognition scene.
So much for that, the skeptic in me says.
And yet as I beheld you floating there
I felt myself grow small, the air grow thin,
as if I were the one adrift in space,
and you the one who might yet pull me in.

Scale

Three weeks before our son was born
you went out east to build a barn
from panels of translucent glass:
set in the middle of the marsh
with nothing close at hand for scale,
the barn might have been large enough
to accommodate a man, or small
enough for him to reach his arms
around it. It took a while to build
the barn: the week you planned to be
away stretched into two. You said
you felt like Odysseus, his wife
and infant son at home, detained
for years beyond his expectations.

I think about Odysseus,
set in the middle of his story,
nothing close at hand for scale:
it's hard to tell if it's his ship
that carries him back home, or he
who carries his black ship back
into harbour. A lot of things are like
that now: these days I carry around
our son, who one day will carry us
around, inside him.

Love Poem

After the child was born, the words fell silent:
withdrew, to form a kind of breathing glade
around this purer version of expression.
So much for words, I thought (and yet, already,
our son is reaching out for "Mum" and "Dad").

What Is, Goes

What is, goes. That is all
we know, on earth as it is, which is
enough, if not all we need to say.

What more is there to say?
Man is in love and loves
what goes, said Yeats, and went away.

Cast a cold eye on his grave:
it's going, too, if slowly. Say
all that you know of life, of death,

and so, in going, make it stay
long enough to say it goes.
Horse and rider passing by,

that is all we need to love.

Notes

The Bather The italicized line is from Richard Wilbur's poem "The Beautiful Changes."

After "Inversnaid" The title refers to a poem by Hopkins.

The Hyll The words that open the second stanza are from Arthur Golding's translation of Ovid's *Metamorphoses*. The italicized phrase is from Monica Kidd's poem "Anything I Can Touch and Everything that Haunts," which appears, alongside an earlier version of this poem, in the anthology *Approaches to Poetry: The Pre-poem Moment*, edited by Shane Neilson.

A Natural Day The title and italicized words are from Marlowe's *Doctor Faustus*.

Death and Taxes The italicized words allude to the closing couplet of Wyatt's sonnet "Whoso list to hunt …": "*Noli me tangere,* for Caesar's I am, / And wild for to hold, though I seem tame."

Counting Rhyme A loose translation of Catullus 5 ("Vivamus mea Lesbia, atque amemus …"). The opening line is borrowed from Marlowe via Donne.

Rushlight The epigraph and italicized line are from *King Lear*.

Telemachy This poem owes its catalogue of fog signals to *The Oxford Companion to Ships and the Sea*.

Impasse The quoted translation of Rilke's half line is M.D. Herter Norton's.

Horse and Train Mogul is the elephant protagonist of Richard Outram's book *Mogul Recollected*.

The Sword of Damocles The epigraph is from Cicero's *Tusculan Disputations*; the poem ends with C.D. Yonge's translation of that line.

Reflection After John Haney's photograph *Weidendammer Bridge, Berlin, November 2004.*

Writ The italicized lines are from Keats's poem "O thou whose face hath felt the Winter's wind ...." The Perrault story is "Les fées," from his *Histoires ou contes du temps passé* ....

Advice This poem draws on found material, from *Sailing Directions to Accompany the Chart of the North Sea* ... (1914), and from the old sea shanty variously remembered as "Come Down You Bunch of Roses" and "Go Down You Blood Red Roses."

Hello Wounded Soldiers Hurts are blueberries; the word appears in the *Dictionary of Newfoundland English.*

Routine This poem is for Tim and Elke Inkster, publishers, of The Porcupine's Quill in Erin, Ontario.

Cleaning Out the Barn The epigraph is from Rilke's *Die Sonette an Orpheus,* section two, poem four. M.D. Herter Norton translates it, "They always allowed room."

Encounter The italicized line is from Jeffery Donaldson's poem "Ultra Sound." Lines 9 to 11 paraphrase remarks by British astronomer Fred Hoyle. Cosmonaut Alexey Leonov was the first person to perform a space walk; the quotation in line seven is from his description of seeing the earth from space.

List of Wood Engravings

1   A Wave Takes Flight   *3*

2   Night Flows Uninterrupted into Day   *23*

3   The Sea Delivers Up the Sun   *45*

4   The Trees Are Coming into Leaf   *75*

Engravings were made by John Haney in the fall and winter of 2012, in response to poems from *All the Daylight Hours*. They were printed from boxwood blocks and are reproduced at actual size.

Acknowledgements

I am grateful to the editors of the following publications, in which some of these poems previously appeared (sometimes in earlier versions): the periodicals *The Alhambra Poetry Calendar*, *The Antigonish Review*, *Arc Poetry Magazine*, *Canadian Notes & Queries*, *Dark Horse*, *Maisonneuve*, *The New Brunswick Telegraph-Journal*, *The New Quarterly*, *Numéro Cinq*, *Parnassus*, *Poetry*, *Poetry Daily*, *Seven Mondays*, and *The Walrus*; and the anthologies *Air* (Alphabet City 15), *Approaches to Poetry: The Pre-Poem Moment*, *Jailbreaks: 99 Canadian Sonnets*, *Poetry Daily Essentials* and *Undercurrents: New Voices in Canadian Poetry*. A number of the poems were printed individually by private presses (Anchorage Press, Daubers Press, and Gauntlet Press), as limited-edition pamphlets or broadsides. "December" was commissioned by Sylvia Nickerson for a limited-edition Christmas keepsake in 2007. "Rushlight" and "Elegy at Jolicure" began in response to essays by Zdravko Planinc ("'this scattered kingdom …': A Study of *King Lear*") and Peter Sanger ("Good as Green"), respectively.

I am grateful to Houghton Mifflin Harcourt Publishing Company, to Faber and Faber Ltd, to Farrar, Straus and Giroux, LLC, and to the Andrew Lownie Agency (for the Estate of Joyce Cary) for permission to reprint the epigraphs to "Beasts," "Spring," and "Daubers." For details regarding these permissions, please see the copyright page.

I owe the time I had to work on these poems to the support of the Ontario Arts Council, the Canada Council for the Arts, the Rooms Provincial Art Gallery, Terra Nova National Park, and, centrally, my family. Robyn Sarah helped me to find a sequence for these poems, and brought her keen ear to the manuscript in the final stage of its making: I am grateful to her, and to publisher Marc Côté. John Haney made and gave the wood engravings that appear as frontispieces to the book's four sections. Many of these poems were written in conversation with his art works. Thanks, as ever, to him — and to all of the friends and family members whose occasions occasioned these poems.

About the Author

Amanda Jernigan grew up in Nithburg, Ontario, and has lived in Ontario, New Brunswick and Newfoundland, working as a writer, scholar, editor and teacher. Her first book of poems, *Groundwork,* was published by Biblioasis in 2011. She and her husband, artist John Haney, now live in Hamilton, Ontario, with their young son and their dog.